Toxic Mold

The Dangers of House Mold

Contents

Introduction

Many people don't consider mold in the home to be a problem; a quick swipe over with a commercial cleaning product and its gone, right? Wrong. It takes more than that to remove mold from your home permanently and while it is there, it can be causing you all sorts of toxic problems.

With the weather changing across the world, more serious downpours and floods happening everywhere, there is no doubt that mold infestations are starting to increase, both in incidences and in size. If you live in an area affected by these floods and extreme wet weather then there is a high chance that you could already be sharing your home with these potential killers.

Mold isn't always obvious; it can grow anywhere that is damp including your bathroom or a damp basement. Chances are, you will already have spotted those but what about the hidden area? Have you had a water leak recently? A leaky roof? Anywhere that water has been able to get in is a potential hotspot for mold. Mold doesn't necessarily grow just where it got wet; one patch can release millions of mold spores that will settle in your home; it could be in your carpets, behind drywall and in anything that is made of wood.

I bet you didn't know that a Christmas tree is able to breed mold either and can release untold numbers of spores into a room. Ever wondered why you get asthma in the winter or allergies when you shouldn't do? One study showed that, when a Christmas tree is put into a room for a period of 14 days, the air quality in that room and, to a certain extent, the whole house, dropped a least 6 times.

But I live in a hot, dry climate, I hear you say. It doesn't matter because, in fact, you could be at more risk. Mold grows everywhere in the desert and can be some of the most vicious forms of mold known to man.

What so many people don't realize is just how deadly mold is. Not only can it make you very ill, it does have the potential to kill. Obviously, how ill you get and what you get will depend on what mold is present in your environment, how long you have been exposed to it for, your age, your health and any other allergies you may already be suffering from.

According to a study of more than 1600 people who had health issues as a result of exposure to mold or fungus, the major symptoms suffered included:

- Pain in the muscles and joints
- Headaches

- Depression and anxiety
- Loss of memory
- Problems with vision
- Fatigue
- Disturbance to the immune system
- Struggling to breath

Yet, despite all that, not all physicians and medical professionals are fully aware of just how dangerous these molds can be and will often misinterpret your symptoms as being something else. Obviously, it helps if you tell them that you have mold in your home but if you are not aware of it, you can't tell them. Because of that, it is important that you are more aware of what is around you and how to take care of to keep you and your family safe from exposure

So, settle in and read on to learn about all the different types of mold that may be in your house, the effect it can have on you and those around you and how to deal with it properly.

Chapter 1: The Different Types of Mold in Your House

Let's start by looking at the numerous varieties of mold that can exist in your house. Each of these molds has the potential to cause one or more serious health risks:

- **Alternaria** – usually found outside but it will also grow in any damp spaces inside, such as your shower or where a pipe has been leaking. It is also commonly found in buildings that have suffered some type of water damage, such as flooding and, scarily, it can spread from one room to another very quickly. Exposure can bring on asthma attacks and allergic reactions
- **Aspergillus** – usually found inside and it can cause several health problems including respiratory infections, allergic reactions, and something called hypersensitivity pneumonitis, which leads to lung inflammation
- **Aureobasidium** – often found outside but may also grow indoors on surfaces that are made of wood, on painted surfaces or on wallpaper. You may also find it on caulking and window frames that are damp. It is black and pink and causes allergic reactions in many people
- **Botrytis** – found growing in high-humidity areas, such as a bathroom with inadequate ventilation, and can cause asthma attacks and allergic reactions
- **Chaetomium** – often found growing on carpet, drywall and window frames that have all suffered from water damage and it smells musty
- **Cladosporium** – commonly found in the home and, while most molds like warmer climates, this one will also grow in cooler ones. It will grow on carpets, and other fabrics, along with wooden surfaces and can cause several respiratory issues.
- **Fusarium** – another mold that can grow in cooler temperatures and is often found on fabrics that have been damaged by water. It causes asthma, allergic reactions, and respiratory infections. Anyone with an immune system that is already compromised is at higher risk of infections.
- **Penicillium** – another mold that grows on water-damaged materials, such as insulation, carpet, wallpaper, and mattresses. It spreads very quickly from room to room and exposure can cause allergic reactions, lung inflammation, and sinus infections. It presents as a blue and/or green color mold.
- **Stachybotrys chartarum** – often called black mold because it has a black slimy look. It is also referred to as toxic mold although it isn't toxic in itself. It becomes toxic when a person comes into contact with the mycotoxins that it produces and it can cause breathing issues, allergic reactions, asthma, sinus

infection, depression, and fatigue. It smells musty and will grow in constantly damp areas, such as around a leaky pipe or in your air circulation duct.

- **Serpula lacrymans** – a yellow mold that feeds on anything wooden and causes dry rot
- **Trichoderma** – usually found on carpets, wallpaper and other damp or wet surfaces. It also produces a mycotoxin that causes similar health issues to Stachybotrys chartarum. More people are allergic to trichoderma than any other mold
- **Ulocladium** – this mold needs a lot of water to activate and grow so it is usually found in water-damaged houses. You will normally see it growing on walls that are wet and is another one that many people are allergic to.

Chapter 2: The Color of Mold

Mold is actually a good thing for the planet because it works to break down all sorts of organic matter but that doesn't mean that we want it in our houses. Mold is responsible for a lot of medical issues and some kinds even have the potential to cause blood poisoning (sepsis) or brain infections. It doesn't matter what color it is, if you see it, get rid of it. The following is a quick guide on mold colors that you may find in your house:

- **Green** – green mold could be any one of the common house molds, with more than a thousand different species of green mold known so far. The color doesn't really tell you very much about this mold
- **Black, brown, grey or olive-green** – these are the common colors of the Cladosporium genus of mold. Outside, they grow on leaves while, inside, they are usually found on insulation, walls and on damp carpets. These are linked to infections of the skin, eye and sinus and, in very rare cases, have been linked to fungal meningitis
- **Blue, white or green** – these are of the Penicillium genus and, yes, these were the molds that were originally used for making penicillin. These are normally found on walls and in food and, if you are sensitive enough, you may experience an allergic reaction
- **Yellow, black or green** – these are likely to be the Aspergillus genus of mold and we breathe these in virtually every day with no side effects. The problem lies with people who already have a weak immune system or a lung problem because they are at risk of Aspergillosis. This causes coughing, inflammation of the sinus and wheezing and, in more serious cases, causes lung cavities or fungus balls in the lungs.
- **Grey or black** – these are likely to be of the Alternaria genus and are commonly found outdoors on damp and musty soil, plants and other areas. It is also found in the house and was found, after a study, to be present in 90% of the house dust samples tested. These molds can bring on asthma
- **Pink** – this is often seen in wet rooms, such as the bathroom, and looks like a slimy pink discoloration. It is not mold, it is a bacterium called Serratia marcescens and it lives on residues of shampoo and soap. It has been linked to respiratory and urinary tract infections. However, this is more common when catheters or respirators are used so usually won't be a problem in your house
- **Greenish-black** – this is the Stachybotrys genus and is the black mold that has long been linked to health issues. It is not a common mold and it is most likely far less dangerous than media reports would like you to believe. It lives on drywall,

plasterboard, dust, lint, and paper that is exposed to moisture on a regular basis and a constant source of moisture, such as a leaking tap, excess humidity, etc., is required for the mold to grow

Chapter 3: What are Mycotoxins?

Mycotoxins are produced by some types of mold and are extremely toxic. Rather than being released into the air though, the mycotoxins are contained within the mold spores and will only be released when the spore gets wet. What this means is, when you breathe in these spores, the mycotoxins will be released into your body and can grow on cavities and tissues, like the lungs. If left untreated, they cause systemic poisoning. Some mycotoxins and their derivatives have been used in antibiotics, as growth promotions and in other types of drugs, while others have been used in chemical warfare agents.

Mycotoxins are responsible for many different health issues in people who have been exposed to them over an extended period. If significant quantities were to be consumed or inhaled within a short time period, they could prove lethal. One of the food items that are at risk of contamination by some kinds of molds is the humble grain, mainly because they are a source of sugar and carbohydrate. If you eat grains or product from grain-fed animals, there is a chance you have already been exposed – it is estimated that mold and mycotoxin contamination already affects 25% of the global supply of food and animal feeds.

Mycotoxins were first discovered in London in 1962 when around 100,000 turkey deaths were attributed to contaminated peanut ground meal. The meal had been contaminated by the Aspergillus genus of molds and fungi and this led to numerous studies on the mycotoxin produced by them.

Mold and Mycotoxin Exposure – Symptoms

Several health issues have been long associated with fungi and mold:

- Fatigue
- Stuffed runny nose
- Lack of sleep
- Rapid weight gain or weight loss
- Hair loss
- Dry skin
- COPD
- Asthma
- Hypersensitivity pneumonitis
- Numb feeling
- Chronic pain

- Leaky gut syndrome
- Blurry vision
- Changes in behavior
- Feelings of rage
- Teeth problems
- Insulin resistance
- Irritable bowel syndrome
- Fibromyalgia
- Toxic encephalopathy
- Diarrhea or constipation
- Nausea
- Abdominal cramps
- Heart failure

Scary isn't it! And even your pets can fall foul of the same symptoms through contamination of their own biscuits.

Mycotoxins and Their Effect on Hormones

In 2011, a study that was published in The Science of Total Environment journal showed that zearalenone, or ZEA, was present in the urine of almost 80% of a group of females from New Jersey who were tested. ZEA is a mycotoxin that is known to disrupt estrogen and the girls, all aged 9 to 10, presented as being shorter than average for their age and less likely to have started developing breasts.

ZEA mycotoxins start life in grain, like barley, corn, oats, rice, wheat, and sorghum but they have been known to travel through the food chain into meat and dairy products and eggs from livestock fed on grain. It is even been found in beer. Researchers in that study showed a link between contaminated food sources such as popcorn and beef with the ZEA levels in the girls' urine.

ZEA derivatives have also been used in oral contraceptives. In 1969 in the USA, farmers began feeding their cattle on these to improve their growth rate and efficiency and converting food to fatten them up. This practice is still in use and there is strong evidence that it can harm humans. Because of this, it is no longer practiced in the European Union, having been banned.

The 10 Foods with the Highest Levels of Mycotoxins

In a short while, I will talk about these foods but first, I want to talk about the one that has not been mentioned – coconut oil. This is one of life's superfoods but many do contain mycotoxins. This is because most are made from dried coconuts and these themselves contain mycotoxin, for the best results, although it may cost you more; try to source your coconut oil from companies that are proven to only use fresh coconuts in their production.

1. **Alcohol**

Alcohol itself is a mycotoxin, part of the Saccharomyces yeast family or brewer's yeast to you. As well as that, we also have mycotoxins from fruits and grains that may have been contaminated. Many producers choose to use these grains and fruit because they are not fit for table use so, if you enjoy an alcoholic drink, you are at risk of exposure.

2. **Corn**

Corn is commonly contaminated with several fungal toxins, including fumonisin, zearalenone, aflatoxin, and ochratoxin. Aflatoxin and fumonisin are linked to cancer, zearalenone is linked to estrogen issues and ochratoxin to kidney problems.

3. **Wheat**

Wheat is also commonly contaminated with mycotoxins, as are the products that are made from the wheat, such as bread, pasta, and cereals. Pasta may be the least harmful because some of the mycotoxins are discarded when you drain off the water it is boiled in. Sadly, there are still traces of mycotoxins, such as aflatoxin, that are heat-stable and fat soluble and infinitely more harmful. With regards to bread, it matters not whether it is organic or not; no matter what type of bread you eat, if it is made with grain that has been in a silo for months on end, there is a high chance that it has been contaminated. One point of note is that gluten intolerance is one of the hallmarks of mold toxicity.

4. **Barley**

Like the other grains that are liable to be damaged by flooding, drought and the processes of harvesting and storage, barely can also be contaminated by mycotoxins. Barley tends to be a staple ingredient in alcohol and some cereals.

5. **Sugar Cane and Sugar Beet**

Sugar cane, as well as sugar beet, are commonly contaminated with fungi that produce mycotoxins and as with other grains, they feed the fungi, helping them to grow faster. All fungi and molds need sugars to survive.

6. **Sorghum**

Sorghum tends to be used in several different products that are grain-based, for animal and human consumption. It is also used in alcohol drinks.

7. **Peanuts**

in 1993, a study was carried out to show that, in the peanuts used in the research, there were at least 24 different varieties of fungi present. This was following extensive sterilization of the outer shell of the peanuts so, if peanuts are a big part of your life, be aware that you are potentially consuming these fungi plus the mycotoxins that they produce as well. The same study showed almost the same amount of fungi inside corn kernels. While you may be considering planting your own to avoid these mycotoxins, it won't do any good if the seed you use is already contaminated.

8. Rye

The same applies to rye as it does with any other grain. On top of that, when you use rye and wheat together to make bread, you add in yeast and sugar and both are food for the fungus to thrive on.

9. Cottonseed

Cottonseed tends to be mostly consumed in oil form but the grain form is used for a variety of animal feeds. Several studies have shown cottonseed to be high in mycotoxin contamination levels.

10. Hard Cheese

How many times have you pulled a piece of cheese out of the fridge, only to see mold on it? These molds stand a very high chance of containing mycotoxins. Each of the fungi that exist on our planet has the potential to produce at least three different varieties of mycotoxin and that means there are thousands of known varieties. Some cheese, like Gouda, is made with a type of yogurt culture rather than fungi and these are considered to be the healthier option.

Chapter 4: The Health Dangers of Mold Exposure

Although I have already mentioned some of the health risks, I want to talk about some of the more serious risks posed by exposure to mold and mycotoxins. Besides mold, we also have to contend with certain bacteria that thrive in the same environments, often the same place as some molds do. The synergy between the mold and the bacteria dictates that bacterial infections are commonplace in those with inflammatory conditions and fungal infections, making treatment more difficult.

According to scientific research, mold exposure has now been linked to some health conditions where the cause of the condition was not known before. The following conditions are now seen to be, at least partly, caused by mold exposure:

- Alimentary toxic aleukia – low to nil leukocytes after food poisoning
- Dendrodochiotoxosis – mycotoxicosis from the Dendrodochium toxicum fungi
- Kashin-Beck disease – bones and joints
- Usov's disease
- Stachybotryotoxicosis
- Cardiac beriberi
- Ergotism – long-term exposure to ergot fungi
- Balkan nephropathy – type of kidney disorder
- Reye's syndrome – brain and liver swelling
- Hepatocellular carcinoma – liver cancer
- Onyalai

While there are a large number of common health issues that may have a connection to mold exposure, the dots simply haven't been connected yet. Many people talk about the dangers of heavy metals in our foods and in the air that we breathe but, in concentration terms, mycotoxins are far more toxic. They also have a far-reaching effect on the biological systems in the human body than heavy metals and pesticides do and this is in part due to the fact that fungi can get by your immune system through a series of rapid mutations, at the same time producing immune-suppressing chemicals.

Mycotoxins are in or on a mold spore and, when ingested, inhaled or touched, can affect just about every organ in the body. Some of the effects of this have been likened to radiation sickness while other are neurotoxic, causing changes in behavior and cognition as well as causing convulsions and ataxia – this affects more than 70% of those confirmed to have been exposed to toxic molds.

Two of the most toxic molds are Stachybotrys chartarum and Aspergillus versicolor. Stachybotrys chartarum or SC is a green-black mold that grows on any material that is high in cellulose, such as cardboard, straw, wood, hay, etc. especially when that material is wet. It does need a constantly damp environment to grow and to release the toxins it contains so, even if you live in an environment where it is present, you may not be affected because it may not be releasing that toxin. Much depends on what the mold is currently growing on, the temperature, humidity, etc. SC spores have been known to survive temperatures of up to 500° F and can also survive acid, bleach and other caustic agents.

When SC mycotoxins are present, they can have a devastating effect on the immune system. The following symptoms have been reported by people with known chronic exposure to these mycotoxins:

- Symptoms of cold and flu
- Asthma, nose bleeds and other respiratory issues
- Loss of memory
- Aching muscles
- Sore throats
- Headaches
- Rashes and dermatitis
- Fatigue
- Hair loss
- Cancer
- Pulmonary hemorrhage
- Autoimmune disease

SIDS and Mold Toxicity

There is also a link between the toxic effects of mold like SC and some health issues in infants, including, diarrhea, acute vomiting, asthma and, in some severe cases, pulmonary hemorrhaging. Research has now shown that it could be far worse with long-term exposure potentially causing death. There is some evidence to suggest that some SIDS cases could even have been linked to exposure to these molds.

A study in 1994 resulted in a public health report in Cleveland Ohio. 8 infants were exposed repeatedly to mold toxins; one died from pulmonary hemorrhage and 5 of the 8 continued to suffer from recurring issues after treatment in hospital. Since that report, there have been a further 45 cases of infants exposed to mold toxins in Ohio and 16 of those children have died. If a child inhales mycotoxins, it can weaken the blood vessels in his or her lungs and, if the exposure continues, it can end in pulmonary hemorrhage and death. This exposure has also been linked to bronchitis, pneumonia, and croup in children.

Aspergillosis

The other highly toxic mold is the Aspergillus genus. These tend to be found more in rotting plant matter like compost heaps. It is also found in air circulation ducts, heating ducts, insulation and even in some foods. Mostly, these are not dangerous but there are a few that can cause serious health issues, particularly in those whose immune systems are already weak, such as asthma sufferers or those with lung disease.

Aspergillosis is the name given to infections that are caused by this mold and this name covers a range of illnesses from mild right up to severe lung infections to infections of the whole body. Invasive Aspergillosis is the most serious one, occurring when the mold gets into the blood vessels, spreading through the body.

Some of the symptoms of an allergy to this are a worsening of asthma, a productive cough, and a fever. There is also the fact that Aspergilloma can grow in your lungs (small balls of fungus) and this can lead to wheezing, fatigue, coughing up blood and weight loss. If allowed to rise in severity, it can spread to other major organs, such as the brain, kidneys, heart or skin.

Symptoms associated with Aspergillosis include:

- Fever
- Chills
- Pain in the chest and joints
- Coughing up blood
- Nosebleeds
- Pulmonary hemorrhage
- Shortness of breath
- Wheezing
- Skin lesions
- Swelling on one side of the face

Other Diseases

Other diseases and conditions that have now been linked to mold exposure include:

- Learning disabilities
- Gastrointestinal disturbance
- Heart problems

- Cancer
- MS
- Fibromyalgia
- A variety of autoimmune diseases

Chapter 5: Identifying and Cleaning Mold Contaminations

It is a given that just about every house will get mold at some point. It is a nuisance, causing black grout in the bathroom, discoloration on the drywall, rots out damp wood and causes black spots on your siding. If that weren't bad enough, we also know that it is not good for your health to be around it. The trick to mold infestations is to stop them before they grow to a stage where they cause harm to human life and to the house. This chapter is dedicated to showing you how to identify the mold and how to get rid of the smaller infestations, as well as how to deal with larger ones.

Minor mold is easy to remove using ordinary cleaning products but the problem lies in when you disturb the mold – then it becomes dangerous, especially if you already suffer from allergies or have asthma. If your mold infestation is out of hand, the best thing to do is call in a professional and have them deal with it.

Identifying the Mold

Mold comes in all shapes and sizes and all colors as well. It grows out of spores that float about and land on a suitable material. Typically, mold requires a temperature of between 40 and 100° F and damp conditions to grow in and that covers just about every dark, and potentially damp place your house contains.

Visible mold is easy to spot. It's called mildew and it begins life as tiny little black spots that, left unattended, multiply into larger patches. This is what you see when your grout in the shower is going black, it's the black stuff you see on damp walls and outside in damp and shaded areas. At first glance, a surface that has mildew on it may just be construed as being dirty so one way to test if it is mildew or not is to dab a little household bleach on the area. If it goes lighter after a minute or so, it is mildew and not dirt.

Mildew will not cause any damage to the structure of your house but there are mods that can rot out the surface they are growing on. If you see an area that looks rotten, poke it with a sharp instrument, like a screwdriver. If the food is very soft or it crumbles, mold has set in and begun to rot it out.

You can often smell large concentrations of mold; it smells musty so check out damp carpets, crawlspaces, walls and any wet wood that may be underneath your flooring. Look for leaks that cause damp areas, such as taps, pipes and a leaky roof. If you find any large areas of mold, clean them up before things get too bad.

Removing Large Mold Infestations

To remove large mold infestations, you need to follow certain precautions and be prepared for some vigorous work.

If you have damp and moldy carpet it must be removed. Before you begin, ensure you are wearing protective clothing, including a facemask and protective goggles, and have an exhaust fan operating at the window.

Cut the carpet carefully into sections of 6-ft by 8-ft using a sharp utility knife. Use a pump sprayer to mist water over the surface to stop spores from spreading and roll up each section. Using a minimum of 6 mm plastic, double wrap each section of carpet and seal them with duct tape, ready for disposal.

If you have large areas of surface mold, like that common to shower rooms and bathrooms, or sidings, you can scrub them away in a very short time using a solution of 1 part bleach and 8 parts water. Unfortunately, the mold will often spread to places that you don't see until you smell the musty mold smell, see crumbling drywall or see the stains.

If you mold infestations that cover several feet, where there are large amounts of water damage or where you get a very strong musty smell, you will need to take extra precautions in cleaning them. As well as not breathing in the spores yourself, you will also not want the mold to infect the rest of your house. Follow these tips:

- Wear old clothing and old shoes that you can either wash thoroughly or dispose of after cleaning up
- Wear protective goggles and gloves
- Wear a P-100 or an N-95 respirator
- Make sure the room you are working in is well ventilated, using a fan in a window. Don't buy an expensive one because it will be thrown away after you are done – you will never clean the spores off it and all you will do is spread them around again when you use the fan
- Tape up the window openings using cardboard or plywood so that the spores can't get back in
- Use a sprayer to keep area damp where you are working to control the spores
- Ensure your air circulation and furnaces are switched off
- Cover up doors and ducts to contain the spores to the room you are working in

If you have mold contaminating your walls, you will need to cut the wall open to get at it. The wall has to be repaired anyway so cut it back as far as necessary to eliminate the damage – go beyond it to ensure there is none left and to allow the entire wall to dry out.

First, poke a hole into the damaged section to locate any wires – you don't want to be cutting through those. Also, make sure the power is turned off before you start cutting.

If the water damage has gone unnoticed or has been left unattended for a long period of time, you will most likely find that rot has set in. Where you can, cut out and replace any of the spongy, soft studs and the wall sheathing. Where it isn't easy to do this, use a wood preservative to treat the area after you have thoroughly cleaned the wood and let it dry it out completely. Then you should fit pressure-treated wood next to the rotten members to give them support.

Mold Prevention Tips

The main way to stop mold from growing is to ensure that there are no damp patches. The very worst contaminations tend to happen in damp attics, walls, and crawlspaces, especially where water has leaked in externally or pipes have been allowed to leak. Also, those basements that do not have good foundation drainage are susceptible too.

The best forms of defense are stopping all leaks, ensuring there is good ventilation in rooms that may get damp, keep your crawlspaces dry and make sure water is routed away from the house foundations. An effective way of stopping it in bathrooms and where you have shady damp areas outside is to use paint that contains mildewcide. Check with your local dealer to see which ones are best.

Cleaning Up and Repairing

Use your vacuum to clean up any debris. The best way is to purchase an extra-long length hose and stand the vacuum outside while you do this to stop the spores from spreading any further. Afterward, clean the vacuum thoroughly, dispose of any filters and replace with new and use the 1-8 bleach and water solution to clean all the attachments and the tank thoroughly.

Any surfaces that have been scrubbed down with this solution should be left to dry thoroughly. Do not wipe the solution off as it will continue to penetrate the surface, killing off any mold spores that may have gone deeper. Concrete floors can be scrubbed down with either a chlorinated cleaner, dishwasher detergent of TSP.

Have dehumidifiers set up to take the moisture out of the air and away from the cleaned areas for at least 3 to 4 days. Then you can check the areas to see or smell if there is still any mold. If there is, give it a good scrub with bleach again.

When you are 100% certain there is no more mold, use an oil-based primer or a pigmented shellac to seal in the surfaces. Give cleaned walls another coat of fresh paint and make sure you use latex paint with mildewcide in it to stop mold from growing again in the future. Always bear in mind that, if the damp or the water comes back, so will the mold.

Cleaning Surface Mold

Surface mold will grow anywhere that is damp, especially on the grout between your shower tiles. These are easy to clean; simply mix together 1 quart of water, half a cup of household bleach and a small squirt of household detergent. Shake well and scrub away. The detergent will help to lift the mold off the surface and the bleach kills it. Simply rinse off the wall and you should find that, although it will return at some point, it won't come back quite so quickly. You can also pick up household mildew cleaner from most stores.

Even when you are doing this, make sure you are wearing protective clothing, especially long sleeves, goggles, and gloves. If a light scrub doesn't remove the mold, reapply the mixture, leave it on there for a few minutes and then have another go.

When all the surfaces are clean and have dried off thoroughly, seal the tile joints using a grout sealer to slow down moisture penetration in the future.

One important word of caution here – NEVER combine bleach with ammonia or with any product that contains ammonia because the result will be a gas that is highly toxic.

Chapter 6: Mold Testing

Mold testing will let you know for definite if you have a serious mold problem in your house. You can do this in one of two ways – call in a professional tester or do it yourself. A mold test will also help you to locate mold that is hidden from sight, it will measure the quality of the air in your house and it will even go as far as to identify the mold species.

It is best to have a professional mold tester do this for you because the results will always be more accurate. They will know how to collect and analyze the samples to ensure correct identification.

Using a Mold Test Kit

That said, you could purchase a mold test kit that will allow you to collect your own samples. This is the cheaper option over having a professional tester which can work out quite expensive. Any samples that you collect will be sent off for analysis to a professional testing laboratory that will then contact you when the results are ready.

While a mold test is able to tell you what is going on in the area at the time, it is worth noting that mold spores move around and they also fluctuate in number. For this reason, you should carry out several tests, at different times and in different parts of your house. This will give you a far more accurate picture of what is going on.

Different Mold Tests

There are 4 main types of mold test:

- An air test
- A surface test
- A bulk test
- A culture test

You should do all three tests since each is different and, on their own, will not give you an accurate picture.

- **Air Tests**

An air test will take a sample of the air to see what the mold spore concentration in your house is. These samples will be examined in a laboratory under a microscope. These tests can tell you if you have a problem with mold even if you can't see the mold. That said, the number of spores in the air changes constantly and, while you may only have a few for the first test, another test can give completely different results altogether.

- **Surface Tests**

A surface test will collect samples from the surfaces in your home to see how much growth and what concentration of spores are deposited around the house. Swabs are used to take the samples, although sometimes other methods, including tape-lifting will be used, and the samples examined in the laboratory.

As with the air test, the results will be different because the mold spores will not be evenly spread over your surfaces. The one thing that a surface test cannot identify is the concentration of the spores in the air.

- **Bulk Tests**

This kind of testing involves the collection of materials from all around the house. This material is then examined under microscopes in the laboratory to determine if there is a problem and what the concentration of mold spores is.

- **Culture Tests**

Culture tests involve the mold particles that have been collected from your house being colonized into larger samples. This allows the laboratory to identify the type of mold in your house. However, the only mold particles that can be grown are those that are still alive.

That said, even dead particles will still cause you health problems and allergies.

Why You Should Test Your House for Mold

There are several reasons why your house should be tested for mold, including:

- You see the signs of mold or you can smell it
- To find out what type of mold is growing
- To see where the mold is growing
- To test the quality of the air indoors by seeing what the spore concentration is
- To make sure all mold has been successfully removed from your home

Signs of Mold

The obvious signs of mold are that you can see it or smell it but other signs come in the form of allergies. Hidden mold releases spores into the air and when you breathe them in, you may suffer an allergic reaction such as a runny nose, sneezing or runny irritated eyes.

Tests will also tell you the quality of the air in your house by detecting the mold spore concentrations. Some people will have the symptoms of mold allergies even when there is no mold in the house and this is because the mold spores can float in from outside or because there was once a mold contamination in the house and a lot of spores have been left   behind.

Testing for Mold After Mold Removal

Once all the mold has been removed from your home, be it by a professional or you have done it yourself, you should run another set of mold tests. These will tell you if your efforts were successful or not although, should you do it yourself, you are less likely to get a 100% positive result on a clean house than if a professional removed the mold.

Testing your surfaces again will tell you whether your cleaning removed it all and air tests carried out a while after the mold removal will also tell you if your home is free of mold spores or if they are, at least, at a safe level.

Chapter 7: How to Combat Mold with Food

The symptoms of mold infection can range from mild to severe and, hopefully, if your symptoms are that bad, you are speaking with your physician and you have told him or her that you have been exposed to mold. By now, you should have identified the mold and cleared it from your house. The trouble is, the effects on your health won't go away quite so quickly but there are certain foods that you can include in your daily diet that will help you to combat the effects of mold. You will have to avoid foods that are high in carbohydrate and high in sugar, simply because mold spores feed on these foods and if you have already inhaled them, all you are doing is feeding them. There are lots of alternatives though and there is a very good reason why these foods are safer for you.

Root Vegetables and Tubers

- **Ginger** – Ginger root is one of the best detoxifiers you can get. It works to increase your circulation, it helps to detoxify your liver and it will stimulate your immune system while soothing any inflammation that lingers in your intestinal tract. There are lots of ways you can include ginger root in your diet, from adding it to a smoothie to chopping it up into a healthy stir-fry.
- **Radish** – Most of us like to add radishes to a salad but not many of us are aware of just how good for us they are. Radishes are packed with properties that kill of yeast and mold. It is fair to say that they are top of the heap in the world of anti-fungal foods. In the last 10 years, studies by scientists have unearthed the fact that radishes contain a plant defensin called RsAFP2 and it is this defensin that destroys yeast and mold on a cellular level. So far, they have not found a fungus that fights this plant defensin and survives because the defensin attacks the cell walls of the fungus, killing it off completely. So, don't stick to just one or two radishes on your plate, eat as many as you can.
- **Garlic** – Garlic is another food that naturally slows the growth of yeast and mold and you will usually notice a change within a few hours of eating it. Garlic has allyl alcohol in it and this obliterates any yeast in its path. And fresh garlic is far cheaper and far more effective than any of the pharmaceutical alternatives that you may see. Again, you can add garlic to your diet in many different ways, even eating it raw.
- **Onions** – In a similar way to garlic, onion is a detoxifier and also contains antibacterial, antifungal and anti-parasitic properties. Onions also work to help flush out any excess fluid in your body and this is good news for all who have been affected by yeast and mold because one of the symptoms is water retention.

Choose onions that have a strong smell and taste as they are far more effective and, where possible, consume them raw.

Herbs

- **Cilantro** – Possibly your best friend if you eat a lot of onion and garlic! Cilantro, otherwise known as coriander, freshens your breath, reduces the infection symptoms and protects you from the yeast and mold. It has anti-inflammatory and anti-fungal properties and, if you already have another disease, such as diabetes or your immune system is already low through illness, cilantro will not only strengthen your immune system, it has also been shown to cause insulin-like activities in the body.
- **Basil** – Basil is a sweet herb with anti-fungal properties that suits any dish. It also works very well when eaten with garlic. It is potent against yeast and mold and when you turn basil into an essential oil, it is even more potent. Add it fresh to any meal.
- **Oregano** – Another herb with a nice taste, oregano has a use in medicine for fighting fungus. According to experts, oregano is 100 times more effective and more potent than the caprylic acid that is a normal ingredient in modern solutions for fighting fungus. This is because of the carvacrol it contains and this is made even more potent when made into an essential oil. Add fresh oregano to any dish.
- **Rosemary** – This one doesn't have any real anti-fungal properties but it is an excellent herb for helping reduce yeast and mold infection symptoms. Rosemary goes great cooked up with any fish or meat dish.
- **Thyme** – Thyme is a great herb for those suffering from lung infections through mold exposure. Again, it is more potent as an essential oil but it also tastes great as a seasoning to most dishes. It is packed with anti-fungal properties and, like the oregano it contains carvacrol. This is a must-have in your fight against yeast or mold infection.
- **Black Walnut** – Rather than the nut, it is the husk and the bark that gets ground up for use in natural healing. Black walnut has an active ingredient known as juglone. This is one of the fastest-acting anti-fungal remedies and is as strong as anything you can get over the counter. Juglone contains antibiotic and anti-fungal properties and also includes tannins, which are known to kill off fungus. The only downside to black walnut is that, because of its potency, it doesn't get on with any other plant.
- **Pau d'Arco** – This is another derivative of a tree bark and this one helps your bowels to loosen up – not in a desperate way, just in a way that makes you feel so much better. It has very potent anti-fungal properties and contains lapachol

which has been proven to slow or stop yeast and mold from growing. Pau d'Arco comes in the form of a tea.

Spices

- **Cinnamon** – Cinnamon is one of the biggest killers of yeast and mold. Its active ingredient is cinnamaldehyde, which is one of the most potent antibacterial, antifungal and antioxidant agents. Cinnamaldehyde has been shown to attack and wipe out yeast and mold infections so don't be tight when it comes to using it. Sprinkle as much cinnamon as you want on your food or add it to hot water with a little honey and drink it.
- **Cloves** – In a similar way to rosemary, cloves do not really have any anti-fungal properties but they are excellent at fighting the damage done by the mold infection and can help you to feel so much better. They contain antiseptic and antioxidant properties but do not allow your pets to come into contact because it is toxic to animals.
- **Cayenne Pepper** – Cayenne pepper works to support the immune system and digestive system naturally. It also helps with digestion of food, cleans toxins, yeast and mold from your bowels, thus easing constipation, and it increases blood circulation and your metabolism, which is good news for those suffering from mold infections as one of the symptoms is constant fatigue. Sprinkle on or in any dish.

Turmeric, Sage, and allspice are still being studied to see what effect they have on mold infections but there are many claims that they are an excellent addition to the diet for fighting fungus infections. Usually, these work best if they are infused with a tea.

Oils

- **Coconut Oil** – Coconut oil is top of the heap when it comes to fighting yeast and mold infections. It contains caprylic and lauric acids, both of which kill most yeasts and molds and help to boost your immune system. Coconut oil is an incredibly versatile anti-fungal solution. You can use it for any type of cooking or baking, rub it into yourself as a lotion, use it as a conditioner for your hair, eat it straight from the jar or use it as an oil puller. This involves swirling a spoon of coconut oil around in your mouth for about 20 minutes and then spitting it out, helping to remove bacteria and toxins from your body. As I said earlier though; do be sure to get the coconut oil that is made from fresh coconuts, not dried.
- **Olive Oil** – Olive oil is one of the oldest known healthy oils and it contains a plant chemical that is called Oleuropein. This has very potent anti-fungal properties and has been shown to stimulate and boost the immune system

specifically where yeast and mold infections are concerned. Olive oil also helps to stabilize blood sugar levels and this is an important factor in halting the growth of yeast and mold because high sugar levels simply boost their growth.

Legumes and Greens

- **Leafy Green Vegetables** – Any kind will do. Nobody can get truly excited about a salad but if you add lettuce and any other green vegetable you can think of, like cabbage and spinach, you will be helping to push toxins out of your body. These toxins are pushed out through your intestines to be eliminated in a natural way. They also cleanse your entire body and work side-by-side with other anti-fungal foods to do their business. Like any plant, green leafy vegetables contain natural anti-fungal properties and, although they are not so intense as things like garlic and radishes, they do make a big difference when you include them on a regular basis.
- **Frozen or Dried Legumes** – Beans are a super food, there is no doubt about it. The more of them you eat, the more chance you have of fighting of mold and yeast infections. That said, don't overdo it because, although they are anti-fungal, you should consume in moderation until the infection has gone. Some of the best to eat are red lentils, chickpeas, black-eyed peas, split peas and organic soybeans. They are full of protein and fiber but do not eat them every day and don't eat too many in one go.

Nuts and Seeds

Any vegetation has some form of anti-fungal properties but not all of them work to destroy mold and yeast infections. The following list of seeds and nuts are pretty much neutral and are safe to eat:

- Brazil nuts
- Hazelnuts
- Cashews
- Almonds
- Macadamia nuts
- Coconut meat
- Flax seed
- Sesame seed
- Poppy seed
- Sunflower seed
- Pecans
- Pumpkin seed

- Pine nuts

Gluten-Free Grain

The following are the safe cereals and bread to eat. These are high in fiber and will help to rid your body of toxins but do only choose gluten-free versions of them:

- Oat bran
- Millet
- Quinoa
- Buckwheat

Vegetables

As I said earlier, all plants have some form of anti-fungal properties so, until the infection has cleared up, you should stick to a vegetarian diet as much as you can. These are the best vegetables to eat to fight off mold and yeast infections:

- Asparagus
- Artichoke
- Avocado
- Brussels sprouts
- Broccoli
- Celery
- Cabbage
- Cucumber
- Eggplant
- Raw garlic
- Kale
- Onions
- Olives
- Rutabaga
- Spinach
- Tomato
- Zucchini

These are all non-starchy vegetables and this means they do not convert into sugar in your body and do not feed the mold and yeast when digested in your stomach. In effect, if your diet consists mostly of these, you will starve the mold and yeast and force it out of your body.

Meat

Keep your consumption of meat as low as possible. Fungi feast on rotten flesh so don't turn your stomach into a graveyard! If you do feel the need to eat meat, only go for whole and organic foods, nothing non-organic and nothing processed. Forget the bacon, spam, smoked meat, lunchmeat and any meat that comes in a vacuum-packed container. These are all full of nitrates, dextrose, sulfates, and sugars, all of which will happily keep the fungus alive and thriving. Stick to consuming beef, chicken, lamb, turkey, and salmon – only fresh foods though, not tinned or packaged.

The foods listed in this chapter are just a quick look at the edible ways of fighting yeast and fungus safely. There are lots more, far too many to mention here. The key to work by is to starve the fungus right out of your body. Don't give it anything that it could possibly feed on. And, when the fungus infection is gone from your body, don't go back to your old eating habits. While that may not have caused the mold infection in the first place, certain foods do, as you know, contain mold spores and you will find yourself right back where you started.

Chapter 8: Dealing with Moldy Food

We have all done it most likely, taken a bite out of a sandwich before we realize that the bread is, in fact, a little on the moldy side. How many of us have thought to ourselves, "now I've got food poisoning!"? Maybe a few of us but is eating a little bit of mold all that bad?

The short answer would be no. You will not die from eating a piece of bread that has a small amount of mold on it. It will be digested like any other food you eat and, so long as your immune system is in good shape, the most you will experience will be a feeling of nausea and you may even vomit but that is only because of the thought of what you just ate, nothing more serious. All that said, mold is not good for you and if you have a mold or yeast allergy then you will likely experience some uncomfortable side effects, including irritated eyes, throat, and nose.

Although the mold commonly found on bread isn't harmful there most definitely are some dangerous molds out there and these are the ones that can cause problems. Some of them produce mycotoxins, poisonous substances that have the potential to cause cancer. Having said that, the contamination is likely to appear further up the food chain that in your kitchen, as these toxins normally only appear in crops of grains and nuts.

1. **Can I Cut the Mold Off?**

The temptation is strong. It's the last piece of bread and you really want it so if you just chop off that moldy bit, it will be fine. Won't it? Maybe but you have no way of knowing if you have removed all the fungal infection when you cut the mold off. Mold spreads its roots like threads down into the food so just cutting off what you can see doesn't necessarily mean you have cut it all off. Best to be safe and not eat any of it. Later, I will provide you with a list of foods and tell you whether they should be discarded entirely or whether you can get away with chopping off the moldy bit.

2. **Can't I Toast it? That Will Kill the Mold**

Actually, heat doesn't necessarily do this. You can, technically, destroy mold when you expose it to high temperatures, the chances of your grill reaching those temperatures is very slim indeed. If it did, there would be nothing left of the bread but a pile of charred remains. And even then, you could not guarantee that the mold infection would be completely gone!

3. **Can I Eat Moldy Cheese?**

There are cheeses, such as the Gorgonzola, that are made with added mold cultures but these molds are able to produce any mycotoxins. Setting those cheeses aside, other cheeses will need to be handled differently if they have mold on them – in short, a hard or a semi-hard cheese can be trimmed but a soft cheese that has mold on it should be discarded altogether.

4. **How Do I Stop the Mold from Forming on the Food?**

There are a few steps that you can take to stop food from going moldy. Cover refrigerated foods securely, either wrap it in plastic wrap or store it in a sealed container. Consume any leftovers inside of a four-day period and do not leave any perishable foods out of the refrigerator for more than 2 hours. The most important thing is to be realistic – if you can't eat an entire loaf of bread in a week then don't buy one. Or buy a loaf, split it and freeze it!

What Happens If My Toddler Eats Mold?

If you have young children, particularly toddlers or infants, then you know that nothing is safe from their mouths, not even a piece of moldy food. Most of the time, there is no need to panic and the effects will likely be nonexistent or, at best minimal. However, just to be safe, keep a close eye on the child for a few hours after the exposure to see if there are any respiratory or digestive issues. If you are at all worried, simply take the child to your doctor.

If your toddler is allergic to anything like this or already has an illness that has weakened his or lungs or immune system then the effects may be more severe. Your child could experience respiratory issues and this may become noticeable in the form of a stomach virus, with fever, cramps, pain in the stomach, vomiting, and diarrhea. In this instance, do get medical help for your child.

Prevention

It isn't always possible to keep things away from your toddler but do make sure that any perishable foods are stored in the refrigerator, preferably in an airtight container. Do not feed your toddler any cheese or bread that has gone beyond its expiration date.

Mold in the Refrigerator

There is a common misconception that foods stored in a refrigerator will not go moldy. Yes, most mold does like it a bit warmer but they can also grow in cooler climates. Mold also like salt and sugar so you may find mold growing on jam, jelly or salted cured meats in the fridge.

Keeping things clean is important. If you have food in your fridge that has been infected with mold, it must be removed immediately otherwise the spores will build up and spread. Use 1 tablespoon of baking soda in warm water to clean out your refrigerator every couple of months. Rinse it with clean water and dry it thoroughly. If you see any mold, (normally black) on the rubber door seals, scrub it off using 3 teaspoons of bleach mixed in 1 quart of water.

Always keep your dishcloths, sponges, towels, and mops clean. If they smell musty, they are spreading mold spores around. If you can't clean them, throw them away.

Buying Moldy Food

You would be surprised how many people get home from doing the shopping only to find that something they just purchased is already moldy. Before you buy anything, check it over thoroughly. Examine any food in glass containers; check out the stems of fresh produce and never buy any fruit or vegetable that is bruised. If you do see mold on any product, tell the store manager immediately.

You will usually find that fresh poultry and meat are free of mold but anything that has been cooked or cured may not be. Look carefully before you commit to buying. There are exceptions to this – some of the salamis, notable Eastern European, Italian and San Franciscan, already have a thin coating of white mold which is safe to eat. What you shouldn't see is any other type of mold. Dry-cured hams also have a mold coating which needs to be thoroughly scrubbed off before you eat it.

Handling Moldy Food

- Never sniff at a moldy food item because it can cause respiratory issues
- If food is coated in mold, throw it away. Wrap it in a paper bag or plastic first and discard into a covered trash receptacle that no animal or child can gain access to
- Thoroughly clean the area of the refrigerator or cupboard that the moldy food was in
- Check other food items around it to see if they have been contaminated. Fruits and vegetables are easy to infect

Moldy Food – What to Use, What to Throw:

Food

- Luncheon meats
- Bacon
- Hotdogs

DISCARD - these foods are high in moisture and may be contaminated beneath the surface. They may also contain bacteria

Food

- Hard salami
- Dry-cured country ham

USE – these already have mold on the surface although this should be scrubbed off before it is consumed

Food

- Leftover cooked meats
- Cooked casseroles

Discard - See Lunch Meats

Food

- Cooked pasta or grains

DISCARD – See Lunch meats

Food

- Hard cheeses

USE - The mold does not normally penetrate far beneath the surface of these. Be sure to cut out about an inch all around the mold but do not allow the knife to touch the mold or you will contaminate the rest of the cheese

Food

- Cheese made with mold

Discard – if they are soft cheeses, such as Roquefort, Brie, Camembert, Gorgonzola, or stilton, throw them away if the mold is not part of the process used to manufacture them. Hard cheese can be dealt with as above

Food

- Soft cheese

DISCARD - See Lunch meats

Food

- Sour cream and yogurt

DISCARD - See Lunch Meats

Food

- Jam and jellies

DISCARD – the mold may be producing harmful mycotoxins. It is not recommended that you scoop out the infected part as the rest of the product may already be contaminated

Food

- Firm fruits and vegetables

USE – Cut at least an inch around the mold spot but do not allow the knife to come into contact with the mold as you may contaminate the rest of the food

Food

- Soft fruits and vegetables

DISCARD - See Lunch meats

Food

- Bread and other baked goods

DISCARD - These are porous foods and they may have been deeply contaminated

Food

- Nuts
- Legumes
- Peanut butter

DISCARD - any food that has been processed without the use of preservatives are a high risk for mold growing on them

Conclusion

Mold is not a pleasant thing, either to see, smell or taste but not many are aware of the very real dangers that it presents. You may not even be aware that you have mold in your house until it is too late. You may have put your symptoms down to something else altogether, as may your doctor.

It isn't too late to clean it up and clear it out and I have detailed some of the ways in which you can do this. If you are at all unprepared for or cannot handle cleaning out a large infestation of mold, I would strongly suggest calling in the professionals to do it for you – if necessary, move yourself and your family out to a safe place until the work is completed.

While not all molds are toxic, it is better to be safe than sorry so do your best to eliminate mold from every area of your life, right down to the foods you are eating and the cloth you use to clean the surfaces with. I promise you that you will notice an incredible change in your health and your house will smell and feel so much better and cleaner than before.

I hope that I have been of some help to you in identifying and removing sources of mold from your house. The rest of this journey is yours and yours alone – only you can keep the mold at bay.

81016978R00022

Made in the USA
Columbia, SC
19 November 2017